# *Too Many* Chihuahuas

**Mary Minjares**
Author

**Abby Stoffel**
Illustrator

**Morgan Michels**
Production Editor

Kitsap Publishing

*Two Many Chihuahuas*
Second edition, published April 2021

Written by Mary Minjares
Illustrated by Abby Stoffel

Copyright © 2021

Hardcover ISBN 13: 978-1-952685-25-5

All rights reserved. No part of this book may be reproduced or transmitted in any form or by any means, electronic or mechanical, including photocopying, recording or by any information storage and retrieval system, without written permission from the author, except for the inclusion of brief quotations in a review.

Published by Kitsap Publishing
Poulsbo, WA 98370
www.KitsapPublishing.com

"For my kids - Robby, Katie, Cindy, Susie, and Tommy - and Dan, my knight-in-shining-armor."
—Mary

"Dedicated to my Mom, Dad, and my friends for supporting me as I illustrated my first children's book."
—Abby

Today is a good day. Every day is a good day for Becket, the big Golden Retriever.

Becket lives alone with his family. They love Becket. Becket loves them. It is a *good* life.

Because today is a good day and yesterday was a good day, Becket knows that tomorrow will be a good day too! Every day is a good day for Becket.

Becket is a good dog.

He likes hugs whenever he wants one.
He likes naps wherever he wants to lay.
He likes walks alone with his family.
He likes special *biscuits* just for him.

Becket always has to do a trick
before he gets a biscuit.

Sometimes he sits ...
Sometimes he shakes hands ...
Sometimes he rolls over ...

... and sometimes Becket has to sit, shake hands, roll over, and *dance*!!!

His family laughs when Becket does silly things and they call him a circus dog.

Today something woke Becket from a very nice nap. Ouch! Something bit his ear!

Something jumped on his face! Becket was surprised! What was happening?

His toes were being chewed on!
Becket's tail started to wag.
In front of him, no ... under him ...
no ... behind him ... were two tiny dogs!

Becket was so happy!
New friends had come to play!

Today was a very *good* day!

There were tiny Chihuahuas everywhere!
They were very fast and very very busy!

Playing with new *friends* was a lot of fun,
but it made Becket tired.

He curled up on his big cozy bed, but he wasn't alone.
Those chihuahuas hopped right up on top of him!

Becket was surprised but he was a good dog,
and they all took a nice nap together.
It was a good day but it was a short nap!

Those busy little dogs were at it again,
and it looked like Becket was their
favorite toy to jump on!

Becket liked to have a snack after a nap.

Maybe he would find a *snack* in his bowl.

Instead of a snack Becket found
a Chihuahua in his bowl!

Becket was very surprised!
He forgot the rule of no barking in the house.
"Woof!", said Becket.

But what else could he do?
There was a Chihuahua in his bowl!
There was a CHIHUAHUA in his BOWL!!!

Becket was a good dog.
He just wanted a little snack and maybe a hug.
Becket liked snacks and hugs.

Becket looked for his family.
There was always room for Becket
to lay his head in one of their laps,
right on top of ... a **Chihuahua!**

There were too many Chihuahuas!
They were eating Becket's food!
They were laying in Becket's bed!
They were standing in Becket's bowl!
And now they were laying in the lap
where Becket wanted to put his head!

What was Becket supposed to do?
He was a good dog!
Now they were laying with HIS family!

With a *sigh*, Becket found a spot to lay down.
It was a spot all by himself, with no
Chihuahuas, and away from his family.

Becket was all alone.
Maybe today was not a good day at all!

Becket fell asleep and dreamed
about happy times with his family.

In his dream there weren't any Chihuahuas.

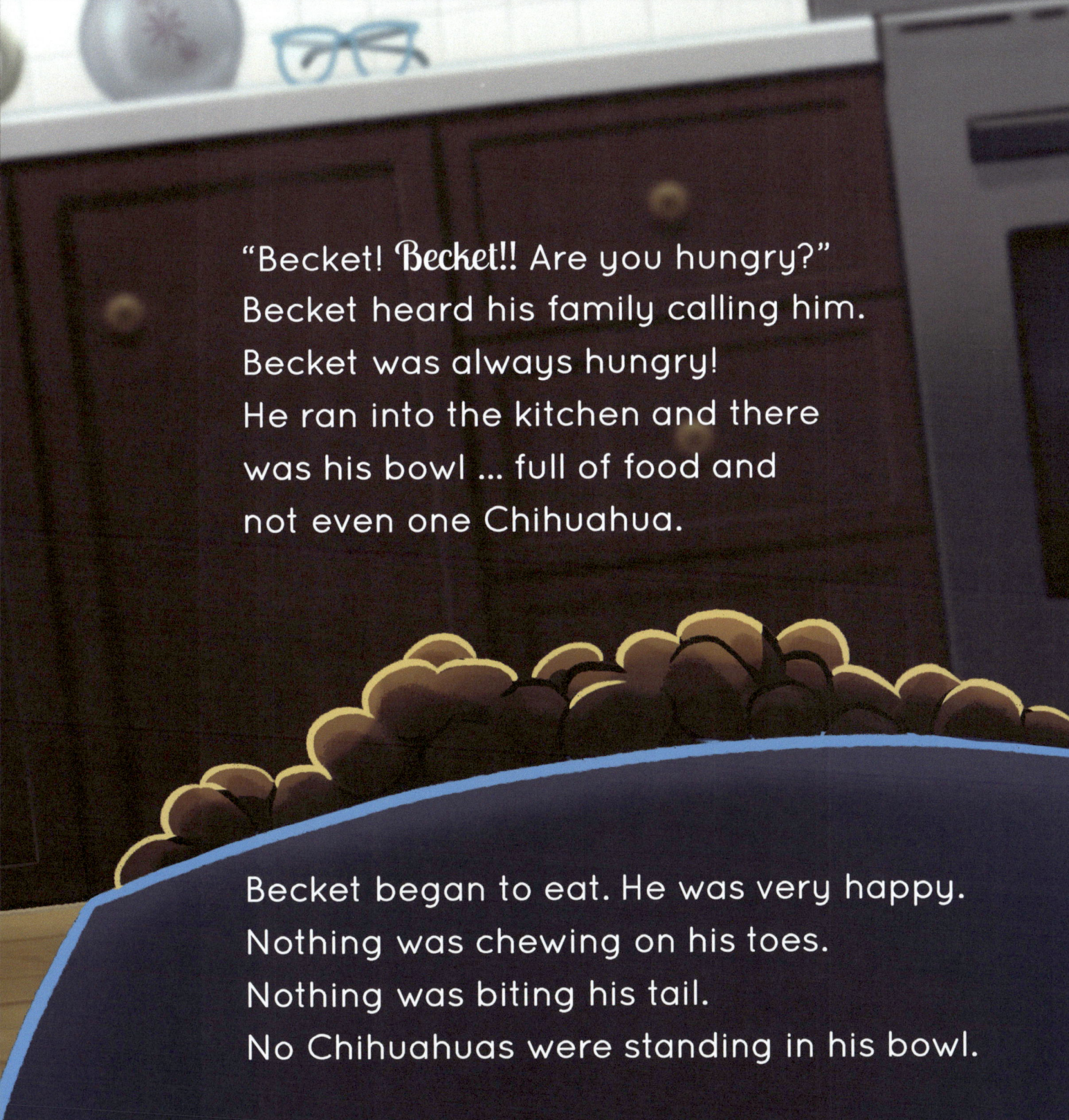

"Becket! **Becket!!** Are you hungry?"
Becket heard his family calling him.
Becket was always hungry!
He ran into the kitchen and there
was his bowl ... full of food and
not even one Chihuahua.

Becket began to eat. He was very happy.
Nothing was chewing on his toes.
Nothing was biting his tail.
No Chihuahuas were standing in his bowl.

Becket stopped eating. He remembered playing and being cozy; maybe the chihuahuas were lonely. Maybe they were hungry, too! Becket went and pushed the door open. The two Chihuahuas ran into the room, right between Becket's legs.

Becket put his nose back into his bowl ...
where the chihuahuas were now standing ...
and shared his dinner.

Too many Chihuahuas?
No, Becket decided,
two chihuahuas was perfect.

He laid down for a nap.
He was not alone.

It had been a good day.

www.ingramcontent.com/pod-product-compliance
Lightning Source LLC
Chambersburg PA
CBHW041501220426
43661CB00016B/1218